OUR LOVE OF Moose

Stan Tekiela

Adventure Publications
Cambridge, Minnesota

Dedication

To Agnieszka Bacal. Moose are as magical as your love for nature.

Photos by Stan Tekiela

Edited by Sandy Livoti

Cover and book design by Lora Westberg

10 9 8 7 6 5 4 3 2 1

Copyright 2017 by Stan Tekiela
Published by Adventure Publications, an imprint of AdventureKEEN
820 Cleveland Street South
Cambridge, Minnesota 55008
(800) 678-7006
www.adventurepublications.net
Printed in China
ISBN: 978-1-59193-690-9; eISBN: 978-1-59193-691-6

Symbol of Grandeur in the Wild 〜

Moose are magical—it's just as simple as that! Their massive size and gentle nature endear them to those of us who seek them out and others who stop to admire them during a chance sighting. I have been studying and photographing moose for three decades and am constantly in awe of this amazing animal. With each encounter I'm reminded that even though they are huge, they move with the grace and silence of a light breeze. It seems that everyone loves moose, and watching one during a vacation is often the highlight of the trip! Along with many people across the United States and Canada, I personally have great respect and admiration for this symbol of grandeur.

Moose: Animals You Can't Mistake

When you see a moose, you just can't help but stop to admire it. The largest and most magnificent member of the deer family, moose are closely related to caribou, deer and elk.

Moose are found all across the Northern Hemisphere from China to Scandinavia and throughout northern North America. However, the common name "moose" is used only in North America. In Europe, moose are known as elk. This can be confusing for people in the United States and Canada because we have a different animal that goes by that name. But regardless—you'll never mistake a moose for an elk.

Getting Ready for Autumn Mating ～≫

Autumn is the breeding season for moose, and it is their most active time of year. This is when females, known as cows, gather together in small groups. Males, called bulls, are mostly solitary, but in the fall they also congregate in small groups.

Females enter the breeding stage at 2–3 years of age. They reach reproductive peak at about 10–12 years and continue to reproduce until they're about 20 years old. Bulls will wander far and wide to mate with these enticing cows.

Which One Will Win?

Only the strongest and healthiest bulls will breed. They are in peak physical condition now after feeding on nutrient-rich green plants all summer. The velvet that covered their antlers has since peeled off, and the antlers are full-grown and massive. They polish them vigorously, thrashing them through the branches of shrubs and small trees.

During breeding season, bull moose assess one another by comparing antler size and will fight if they have a similar body size. Approaching each other with stiff legs, they slowly rock their heads back and forth, displaying their antlers while considering their opponent's. Pushing their antlers together slowly, they put their weight of up to 1,400 pounds into a full-body shoving match.

Will She Pass the Flehmening Test?

During the mating season, bull moose check for fragrant hormones released by cows by using an auxiliary olfactory sense organ, called the Jacobson's organ, located in the roof of the mouth. With an outstretched neck, a bull will approach a cow from behind and sniff. He must get close, because detection of the nonvolatile chemical cues requires direct physical contact with the source of the odor. Then the bull turns, raises his head and curls his upper lip as though he's sniffing the air. This is called flehmening. Chemical stimuli transmitted to the brain (hypothalamus) allow the flehmening bull to determine if the cow is ready for breeding.

A Genteel Approach and Advance

In September and early October, bulls often walk many miles each day in search of receptive cows. With their minds on breeding, they don't eat as much now and life is more physically challenging. Cows are ready to breed for only about 24 hours. Regardless, a bull will draw near to one slowly. If she is receptive, he will rest his head on her rump. If she accepts his advances, they will breed. Afterward, the bull moves off to find another receptive cow.

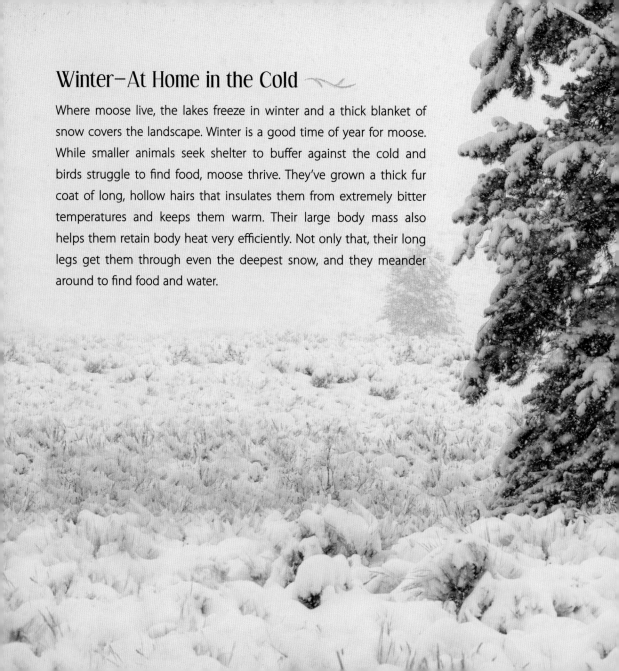

Winter–At Home in the Cold

Where moose live, the lakes freeze in winter and a thick blanket of snow covers the landscape. Winter is a good time of year for moose. While smaller animals seek shelter to buffer against the cold and birds struggle to find food, moose thrive. They've grown a thick fur coat of long, hollow hairs that insulates them from extremely bitter temperatures and keeps them warm. Their large body mass also helps them retain body heat very efficiently. Not only that, their long legs get them through even the deepest snow, and they meander around to find food and water.

Browsing Twigs and Other Munchies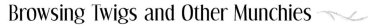

Adult moose need to consume about 45 pounds of food daily. They feed on the most abundant and nutritious plants available, such as fresh green plants, woody twigs, moss and lichens. Aspen, willow, birch and alder leaves are their prime foods, but they also eat tree bark. Moose browse trees and shrubs by grasping twigs and small branches with their lips. They lack upper incisors but bite effectively with their flat, bony upper palate and sharp lower incisors. Jerking their heads back, they rip off an entire twig, leaving a ragged stump. Moving from one feeding area to another, moose alternate between feeding and resting about 7–10 times per day.

Appetites Through the Seasons

Moose enjoy different diets in each season. In spring, they concentrate mainly on sodium-rich aquatic plants. A moose will dip its head underwater to grab a mouthful of lush greens. Lifting its head slowly, it munches and swallows as water drips all around. Many moose never submerge their heads deep enough to get their ears wet. Others dive 20 feet down to gather plants from the pond bottom.

During early summer, moose switch their diet and start to feed upon maturing, nutritious, terrestrial green plants, including grasses, sedges and forbs (flowering plants). Others eat these foods in late summer. In autumn, bull moose eat far less than usual, as their appetite is suppressed during the breeding season.

What's New on the Winter Menu?

Moose have the ability to survive on just a meager supply of twigs during winter, with woody twigs from shrubs making up the main part of their diet.

The way they eat these foods relates to how the common name "moose" came about. The Algonquian Indian name moos means "he strips off" and refers to how moose get leaves, twigs and bark off plants and trees when feeding.

Chewing the Cud After Meals

Moose have a four-chambered stomach. Food is fermented in the first chamber and nutrients are extracted in the others. Once they finish feeding, they sit down to rest. While resting, they regurgitate a small wad of partially digested food and "chew the cud." You can actually see the bulge of the regurgitated food (cud) moving up and down the throat during this time. They chew the cud for a little while and then swallow it. Moose almost completely digest their food and extract all available nutrients, leaving only small round pellets behind.

A Nose for Knowing

Moose have a keen sense of smell. Just looking at the size and shape of the snout tells you that this animal's ability to gather and identify different odors must be remarkable! Some people think moose use their noses to guide them to the most beneficial plants for their health. The enhanced capability also helps them detect approaching danger. In addition, cows use odor to identify their babies, making smell a vital bonding agent between mothers and their offspring.

Ears Going This Way and That

Moose have large ears and excellent hearing. They can rotate their ears in any direction and also move them independently from each other. The abilities enable them to listen to sounds from in front and behind them at the same time. Their agility serves them very well when they listen for predators. It also helps mother keep an ear on junior while she focuses on another direction.

Here's Looking at You

Moose may have a first-rate sense of hearing, but they don't have tremendous eyesight. The size of their eyes in proportion to their heads indicates that they have only average sight. The placement of their eyes on the sides of their heads is even more telling. For a moose to see something directly in front, they need to bulge their eyes and strain to look forward. Most of the time they have a large blind spot in front but relatively good vision on each side.

Like other deer family members, moose have reduced color vision with good sight in shades of white, black and gray. They see movement and motion the best, which makes perfect sense since sighting approaching predators is the most important thing to see.

The Crowning Glory of Moose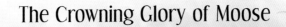

Most everyone associates moose with their distinctive antlers, but only bull moose grow them. The more mature, healthy and dominant the bull, the larger the antlers. Diet and age determine antler growth rate, size and, to some extent, shape. Normally it takes up to 5 months for the broad, flat (palmate) antlers to grow to full size, with the growth period occurring once each year, before the autumn breeding season begins.

Alaskan moose, which are the largest of moose, grow a set of antlers with a spread upwards of 80 inches—that's nearly 7 feet across! Made of calcium, antlers have the same composition as bone and can weigh up to 40 pounds each. This means that some bulls are carrying around up to 80 pounds of weight on their heads!

Drop Those Antlers!

Bulls display their antlers mainly as decoration but also to spar and fight. When shoving during a fight, so much pressure is placed on the antlers that the points, called tines, sometimes break off.

When breeding season ends, the antlers drop off. Each antler detaches within hours or days of the other. The layer holding the base to the head shrivels, loosening the connection. Usually a bull just quickly shakes his head, and off pops the antler. Other times he runs his antler into a shrub or tree to knock it off. In a few days a soft velvet patch covers the stump (pedestal) and a new antler starts to grow.

Aah, It's Finally Spring . . .

Peace and serenity washes over the meadow where the moose cow lives. The dark, cold days of winter are behind her, and she can choose different, more nutritious foods and move about more freely. With a wholesome and abundant cuisine, she doesn't need to feed so much now or walk as far to find sustenance.

She starts to shed the long hairs of her winter coat and her thick undercoat. She is now heavy with a developing baby moose (calf), and she will soon give birth. The twigs and bark she ate this winter provided her with the building blocks to support the growth of the little one within.

Out and About in the World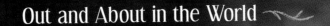

In early spring, after nearly 8 months of gestation, the expectant mother moves away from the other cows to give birth to 1 calf (sometimes 2). Adult cows weigh up to 1,100 pounds and are tall and lanky, standing about 7 feet tall at the shoulder. Newly born calves weigh only about 30 pounds and are small enough to easily walk under the mother without touching her belly. Babies walk within hours of birth and follow their mothers around for short distances in the meadow. They spend much of their time resting after feeding on their mother's nutritious milk.

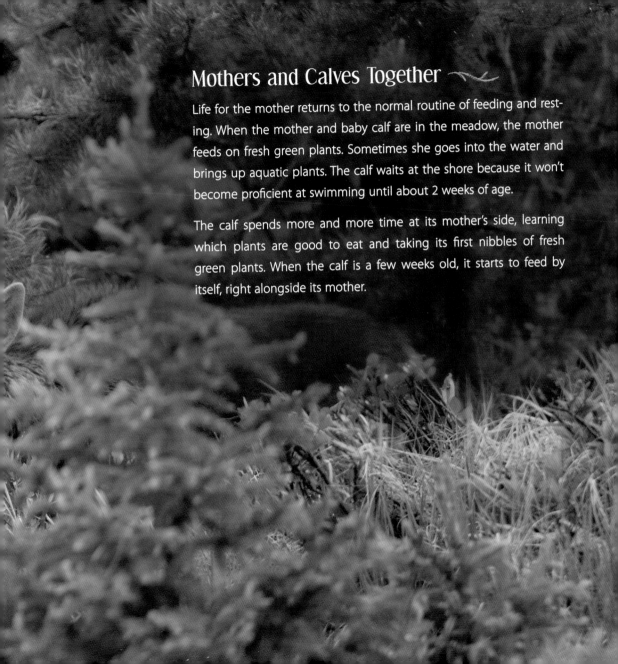

Mothers and Calves Together

Life for the mother returns to the normal routine of feeding and resting. When the mother and baby calf are in the meadow, the mother feeds on fresh green plants. Sometimes she goes into the water and brings up aquatic plants. The calf waits at the shore because it won't become proficient at swimming until about 2 weeks of age.

The calf spends more and more time at its mother's side, learning which plants are good to eat and taking its first nibbles of fresh green plants. When the calf is a few weeks old, it starts to feed by itself, right alongside its mother.

Watch Out for Predators!

Each morning the sun dapples the meadow with rays of warmth and light. The mother moose keeps watch, with eyes and ears alert for bears, wolves and other large predators on the lookout for newly born and highly vulnerable moose calves. Even though a 5-day-old calf can outrun a human, young calves are still not fast enough to dart away from a determined animal. Instead, calves will hide in tall meadow grass and remain motionless for hours when danger is nearby.

A moose mother can be aggressive toward wandering predators, often approaching and driving them off before they discover her calf. Her large size and powerful kicking hooves can intimidate a lone wolf or small bear. Unfortunately, her defense isn't always successful against larger, hungrier animals or wolf packs.

Making It to Adulthood

Young calves grow quickly and can gain upwards of 2–3 pounds a day just on mother's milk. They are weaned at 6 months of age, but that doesn't stop them from trying to continue nursing. By this time, calves weigh over 300 pounds!

The first 3–4 years of life are difficult for young moose. Some of the problems they face besides predators are lack of proper nutrition, accidents (such as a broken leg), moose hunting season and other types of contact with people.

Only around 50 percent of all moose survive to adulthood. After 4 years of age, moose tend to live long lives of upwards of 20 years.

Lives Complete with New Beginnings

Just before the upcoming mating season, the mother moose needs to push away (disperse) the calf that was born during spring. She must do this to keep her calf safe from the big bull moose that will come calling soon. Young moose are dispersed at 12–16 months of age. Young males move farther away, while young females remain close, often sharing the same territory with their mother.

Year after year, the quiet meadow in the forest bears witness to the birth, growth and life of another generation of magnificent moose.

Observation Notes

Date:

Date:

About the Author

Naturalist, wildlife photographer and writer Stan Tekiela is the author of the popular Our Love of Wildlife book series that includes *Our Love of Loons* and *Our Love of Hummingbirds*. He has authored more than 165 field guides, nature books, children's books, wildlife audio CDs, puzzles and playing cards, presenting many species of birds, mammals, reptiles, amphibians, trees, wildflowers and cacti in the United States.

With a Bachelor of Science degree in Natural History from the University of Minnesota and as an active professional naturalist for more than 25 years, Stan studies and photographs wildlife throughout the United States and Canada. He has received various national and regional awards for his books and photographs. Also a well-known columnist and radio personality, his syndicated column appears in more than 25 newspapers and his wildlife programs are broadcast on a number of Midwest radio stations. Stan can be followed on Facebook and Twitter. He can be contacted via www.naturesmart.com.